CROSSOVER VOICES
whispers, shouts, echoes

Words from homeless people and primary school children

"What would you do in my situation?" - Jed

Acknowledgements

Crossover Brighton Press gratefully acknowledges the contributions of homeless people and school children at Mile Oak Primary School to *Crossover Voices*. With thanks also to sculptors Daniel Laurence and Frank DaCosta for making the Crushed Can Cross and to Martin Smith for the foreword.

Crossover Voices: whispers, shouts, echoes

Words from homeless people and primary school children

British Library Catalogue in Publication Data
A catalogue record for this book is available from the British Library
ISBN 978-0-9955016-0-7

First published in Great Britain in 2016 by Crossover Brighton Press, Brighton, UK

Typeset by Woking Print & Publicity

Designer Richard Woods

Managing Editor Linda Bolton

Editor Evlynn Sharp

Sculptors Daniel Laurence and Frank DaCosta

Photography Evlynn Sharp

Artworks by kind permission of Paige, Mitch, Peter, Ady, John, Mile Oak Primary School

Printed and bound by Woking Print & Publicity
The Print Works, St John's Lye, Woking, Surrey GU21 1RS
Tel: 01483 884884

Artwork: Numbers in italics refer to pages in which artworks appear:
School children, *covers & title page, 6, 13, 30;* Ady, *4;* Mitch, *5;* Paige, *11;* John, *17;* Peter, *20*

Crossover Brighton provides food, support and other services to homeless people. Please visit the website for information: www.crossoverbrighton.org   Registered charity number 1153475

Foreword by Martin Smith

Crossover Brighton's Dave and Linda are the real deal.

Every now and then you meet people who don't just talk about their crazy ideas but they actually end up doing them! These two amazing humans are a perfect example of this way.

If they have a heart to feed people on the street they'll go and buy a burger van, if they need to give homeless guys a job they'll lease a charity shop, if they meet someone who needs a bed for the night they'll try to provide one, and if they need to help people financially then they'd probably sell their house.

This book is another one of their beautiful ideas.

Using creativity to break our hearts rather than just inform our minds.

Helping to give people a voice who do not have a voice.

Encouraging children, the future stakeholders of society, to bring change at every level, and help bring those who are lost out of the shadows.

That's what Dave and Linda do best. Find people who have been discarded and give them hope. It's a crazy concept but they see it happen every day!

Martin Smith
English vocalist, guitarist, songwriter, and producer
June 2016

Streets ePanic

7.15am. Alistair - a homeless man - shoulders his rucksack.

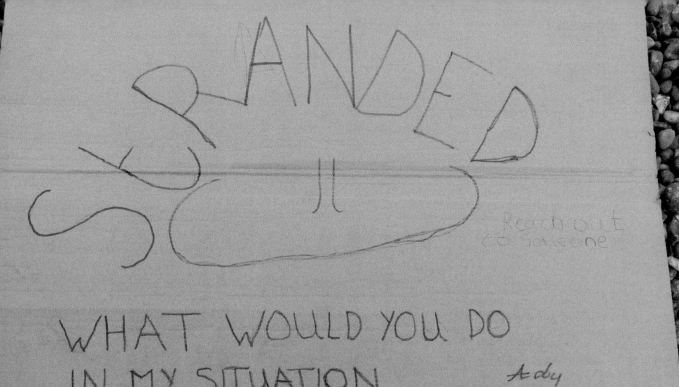

WHAT WOULD YOU DO
IN MY SITUATION
?

Ady

STRANDED

Definitions of stranded: isolated; left behind in a difficult position;
stuck somewhere with no way of going elsewhere...

"Reach out to someone." – Ady

WHITE DOG

Shaun

A white dog sitting calm as hell
But he's so angry with the frustration
No one can tell. The hell inside him
Awaits to pop. That when he kicks off,
No one knows where he will stop.

On top the panic kicks in,
People's comments, but they don't know him,
Up to the chin when he can't take no more,
He seeks sanctuary with the things he adores.

A clown in training when at your weakest
They will draw you in and make you think:
They are the meanest,
While all along promising you the
Earth. Then take away what is left
Of your self worth.

Chosen new identity. I tried to gain
But in the sunshine thunder pouring rain
The fire came. I tried to put it out
But all I could do was run,
The fire had overcome me,
The fire had almost won.

I got so low that I wanted to end my life
Where it took so long for me to realise
People like that are weaker still
Manipulating with threats of a kill
Should you turn to Old Bill.

I finally come to my senses as I realise
That everyone is born and dies,
So I should face my demon whatever the outcome
And show them all who's Number One.

And back to the life I so belong.
True. Meaning.
White dog sitting.
A clown in training.
Chosen new identity.

Mitch, Fire

5

STRANDED

WILL I FIND A HOME?

Heidi, age 11 (Mile Oak Primary)

Here I am lying against a garage door, my cardboard giving me warmth.
I look around and small stones fly into my eyes giving me a painful sting.
The sun is just dipping under the horizon.
I hate the dark.
As I make myself comfortable, I hear giggling coming from behind some cars.
It's a group of young children.
They're mimicking the way I look using their hands to pull their faces in strange directions.
I'm filled with jealousy.
If only they could see how lucky they were.
By now, it's very dark and the same feeling I have every night came to me.
Worry.
Would I wake up tomorrow and see daylight?
Will someone help me?
Will I ever find a home again...?

Mile Oak Primary school children, words written on cardboard.

LEAVING

Ashton, age 11 (Mile Oak Primary)

I left without saying bye to my sister.
I was driving to Somerset when I saw Lucy
On a street, lying there. I was so angry
She never told me she was kicked out of her flat
Three months back. I left her. I was 18 at the time.
I'm now 21. I regret this so much. I wish I could find her...

WALK OF MY LIFE

Philippe

I am a man who is desperate to be a better person,
At the end of my walk of life;
On my journey, I met different walks of life.

I preach peace and love –
Not to hold hate in your heart.
I preach love to make you feel better.

I find on my journey empty people
Who just want someone to listen,
They walk away with a smile
And visit me every day;

I have helped people to not hate and to forgive,
To preach love and not to worry about things;
Don't worry about tomorrow.

I have saved a man from being stabbed.
The victim had wounds to his face, a bolt in his head.
I believe I was meant to be here. God kept me here,
On the pavement, on my cardboard,

So I was ready at the right time;
We have now become friends.
His first visit after changed my day.
He hugged me.

Linda Bolton and Philippe
discuss his "walks of life"
in a city alleyway where
he sleeps rough.

Streets
Want me
Back

A homeless man on his way.

THIS WAY
Steven

Long night
Short day

For to walk
This way
And that

Migrate
To the water hole
Church

Doctor
Sick notes

Squat
The lot

One eye open
Not had
Day's sleep

Cold
Nice
Face

NEAR THE BEACH
Erin, age 8 (Mile Oak Primary)

I left without saying goodbye.
My first day of not having a home was really good.
First I went up near the beach and sat down with my dog, Harry.
A few people came across, gave me a packet of mini doughnuts,
And a book. The people walked away when I said thank-you.
The book title was *The Book Of Life...*

✶✶✶

There is a big journey ahead. Will I ever get another home?
Will I ever find a home? Where is my family?
Where are my memories? I think I like this spot.

STRANDED

THE DEPTHS

Shaun

Walking through the depths of time,
Guided by a hand but it isn't mine,
In time where I hope to find in place
('God forbid, man') the human race
To taste though we'll never know what's going on,
With longing to go back before it did ever
First go wrong.

The same old song yet a little out of tune,
I was born with nothing in my mouth;
That is something you and your silver spoon
Could never come to understand;

In a land far and wide
Come let the light shine on in;
I have been so blind.

Philippe's boots

BEING HOMELESS

Paul

What gets me being homeless;
When you are tired, you sit
On the side of the pavement,
The Police hassle you, 'Move on!'

Some of the Public treat us like dirt,
Look at us as if to say, 'You are a bit of dirt
On the floor.' They just walk off.

It would be nice if people stop and say,
'Hello.' Just, 'Hello.' Brightens your day.

"And the King shall reply, 'Truly I tell you, whatever you did for one of the least of these brothers and sisters of mine, you did for me.'" – *Bible (New International Version), Matthew 25:40*

John helps Crossover Brighton clean up after street kitchen work.

9

REFLECTIONS

Paul (with Chico his dog)

A child passing by
Gave me a stone he made –
The stone with a person on it,
An object; and it made my day.

It's not that I want money –
It's nice when someone stops
To speak and say, 'Hello.'

HERE?

Paul (with Chico)

Here? A hard question.
It's my own fault. Drug problem.

Watching people go by
Is like watching the TV –
Watching from the outside.

I'm not invited
To the party of life.

CARDBOARD CITY

Mia, age 10 (Mile Oak Primary)

Here I lie shivering in the cold
The wind like a big slap in the face
My pillow only a bit of rubbish
My mattress only a bit of cardboard
My duvet nothing
I sit here waiting for summer
Waiting for warmth
Waiting for happiness

"The doorway...is a new thing for me."

– Paul

Linda Bolton reaches out
to Paul in a doorway.

STREETS

Streets & Panic disorders

Streets Want me Back

CRAZY

Gold Wet

PAIN

fear

Love Rise Blind

Everything is always Changing

STREETS

Paige

Streets want me back

Streets –
Panic disorders
Shakes
Changing

Streets –
Cold
Wet
Pain

Streets –
Crazy
Fear
Food

Streets want me back
Streets – pain, fear, panic
Streets –

Everything is always changing

STREET LIFE

Danny Boy, The Prodigal

In time I come to realise
How to survive
Become streetwise
Graveyard, doorways
On the stairs, I give up
No one cares
The loneliness, emptiness
At looking back
Wandering aimlessly
Who needs a map
No one can take
My thoughts from me
My beautiful wife
My family
The things that keep my sanity
Walking up and down the street
Looking in restaurants
Do people really eat?
Wandering on from town to town
Always hungry, always down
No respect, no dignity
My reflection in windows
Is it really me?

Phil's boots reflect the wear and tear.

An outcast running
Hiding, insecurity and fear
Can't handle people
Please don't you come near
People are looking at me in distrust
I look like a vagrant no one can trust
My Army days were full of pride
Now, unshaven, bedraggled
Up alleyways must hide
People are passing like ships in the night
Must hide with my bottle
Must keep out of sight
Some people are cruel
They don't really care
I pray for the ones with the evil stare
O dear Lord now I understand
The meaning of the footprints in the sand

CRAZY

CARDBOARD CITY?

Jessica, age 9 & Poppy, age 10 (Mile Oak Primary)

Here, is my home. Here I am, scared I will lose all my valuables.
Here I am, living a life I don't deserve.
I feel scared at night, drunken people could rob me or beat me up.
Here is where I sleep with my head against a garage.
I will live here for the moment
Then I will have to move on to another place
As I'm not supposed to be here.

Here I am scared but happy.
I have my bestie so I feel safe.
Here is where I sleep with my head against a garage.
Here is where I am for the moment
But I will surely get moved on as this place is public.
Here is my life – literally,
Have a piece of cardboard and a jacket
And a sleeping bag...

THE COAT

Edette

I had never met Street people.
All my family are Government; Military.

All my family died.

Someone offered me a second-hand coat,
I said I wouldn't be seen dead in it...

It was beneath me...

But when it got really freezing cold,
I came back for that coat.

"Me, my best friend
and pieces of cardboard.
What more could I ask
as a homeless person?"
 – Jessica and Poppy
(Mile Oak Primary)

MY MEMORIES...

Brian

I've gone from thief to Prince –
The Argus called me "a Prince".

I want to write a book
Called *The Other Side Of Justice;*

My memories of my wife,
My memories of...

The heartache and the misery
To loved ones who are the victims,

And also the criminal
Whose parents and loved ones suffer.

*Saturday morning,
7.30am. Brian walks
towards Kitty, the
Crossover Brighton
mobile kitchen van.*

MONOLOGUE

Amelia, age 10 (Mile Oak Primary)

I'm Ellie. I live on the streets.
And I don't like seeing people walk past me
With their expensive designer outfits;

I lay on the hard cobble floor
Thinking about why people ignore me.
And I think I'm homeless...
The words zoom through my head,
Making me anxious.

I believe in myself.
I think at some point
I can live a happy, healthy life.

People stare at me
And look away.
They don't care about me.
I have to battle through this
On my own...

QUOTE / BIBLE:

"He raises up the poor from the dust;
he lifts the needy from the ash heap
to make them sit with princes and
inherit a seat of honour. For the pillars
of the earth are the Lord's and on them
he has set the world." – *Bible (English
Standard Version), 1 Samuel 2:8*

STREETS

ALL IN PLACE

John

I've got everything
In my place –

Washing machine,
Dryer, cooker,

But I can't live there.
I've slept on the streets

For a few nights,
And I'll get used to it.

A MONOLOGUE

Oliviya, age 10 (Mile Oak Primary)

I remember arriving at KFC,
Hungry. Thirsty.

The next day I saw someone
Walking towards me
With four big boxes of chicken wings
And three cups of drinks,
He handed it over.

And saying *THANK YOU*,
I would eat and drink
When I need it...

"Follow the food..." – Stephen

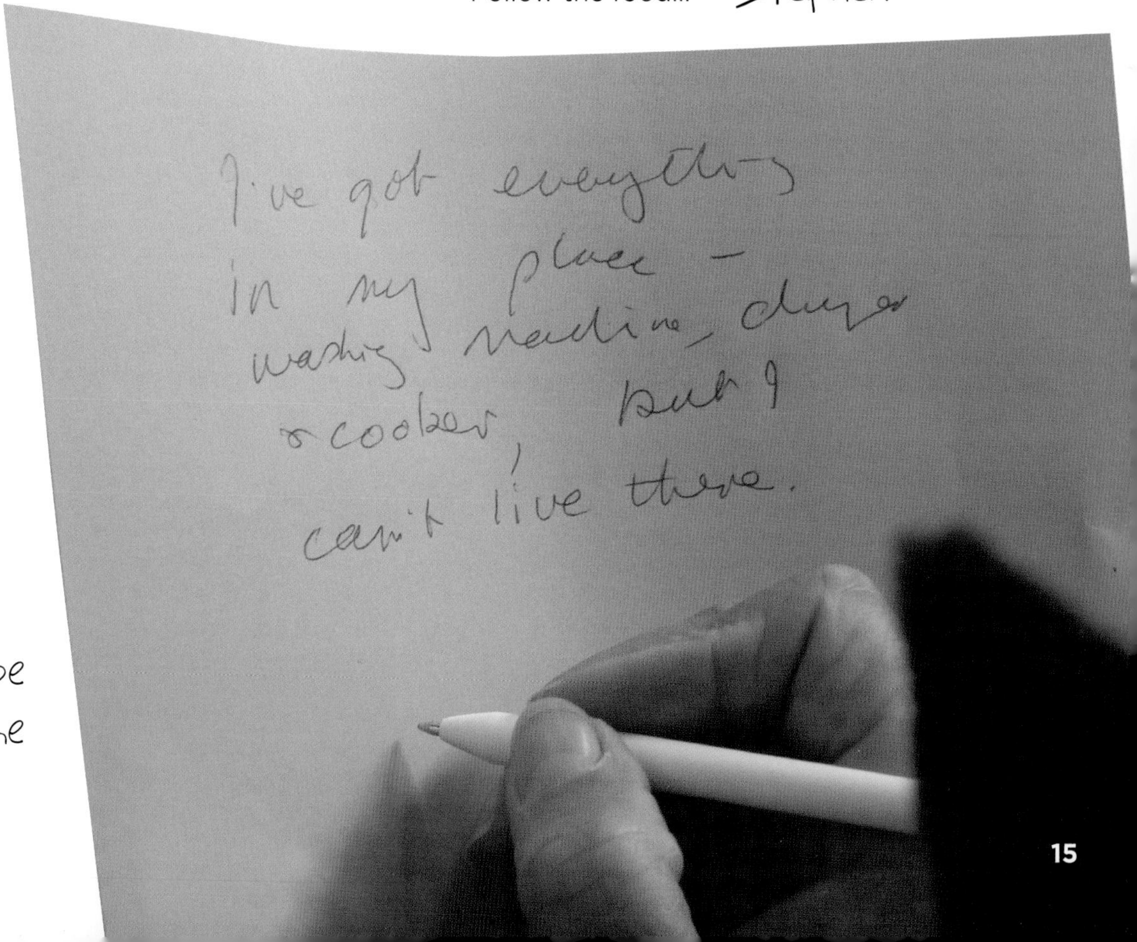

Linda Bolton becomes a scribe for John as he creates a poem about his place.

I've got everything
in my place –
washing machine, dryer
& cooker, but I
can't live there.

15

THIS PRECIOUS, THIS HERE

Cheryl

Precious to me is...
My children,

A roof over my head,
And my God.

God is someone
I can talk to.

And here,
Here...

Totally degrading here,
On the street.

I love and miss my children.
I forgive them.

CARDBOARD CITY

Oscar, age 10 (Mile Oak Primary)

I'm a poor empty soul! It's deadly here!
Every second I have the risk of getting run over.
I NEED FOOD, MONEY, WATER.
I'm a poor sleepless soul.
When I walk my feet get bruises.
Buses crawl.
SAVE ME.
OUCH!
Here I sleep – stones digging into into my back.
CRASH
BOOM
HELP
DEAD INSIDE...
THIS IS A NIGHTMARE
I'M INVISIBLE...
AM I MEANT TO BE LIKE THIS?!

QUOTE:

"I am a mother of a homeless daughter age 25.
I feel despair, hurt, anger, and have shed many
tears. I hear judgement that hurts and is so unfair.
As with our daughter, every homeless person has
a story to tell and a voice to be heard."

- Emma

6.30am. A doorway that is also a place to sleep for a night. Linda Bolton speaks with Cheryl who talks about her family and life on the street.

STREETS

TODAY, TOMORROW

Daisey

Today is treacle,
Foggy,
Heavy.

What will tomorrow hold?

Today I can't walk.
Will you give me a crutch, God?
To help me walk.

Tomorrow?

MONOLOGUE

Zoe, age 10 (Mile Oak Primary)

I left without saying goodbye
To my little girl.
I miss her so much.
Her name was Amy.

It's all my fault.
I should have tried harder
To get clean.

Oh yeah, I'm 26 years of age,
And I'm homeless –
I lost my job five months ago.
I got kicked out of home
Four months ago.

I was brought up in care.
I've never met my Mum.

John is on the streets thinking of his children, echoing Emma who lost her child to the streets.

CARDBOARD CITY

Hannah J, age 9 (Mile Oak Primary)

Here I am just me
And this tiny piece of cardboard

Nothing to do
Nothing to eat

Just me
And this card

I have laid here for weeks
Thinking

Where to go
Next...

I have nothing
Absolutely nothing

Last week I got robbed

Robbed
By the wind...

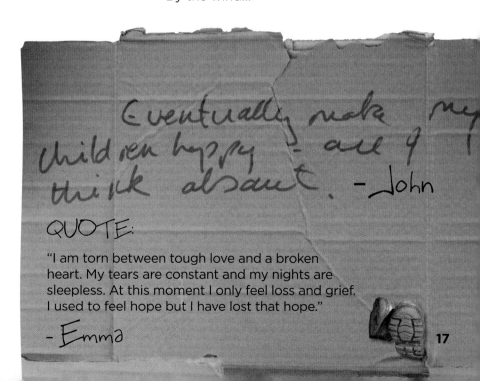

Eventually make my children happy is all I think about. – John

QUOTE:

"I am torn between tough love and a broken heart. My tears are constant and my nights are sleepless. At this moment I only feel loss and grief. I used to feel hope but I have lost that hope."

– Emma

17

STRUGGLES

"I want people to see the real me. The real me is truthful, honest, kind, caring, compassionate."

— Phoenix

"It's not easy out there, and now I'm really struggling."

— Paul

18

THE STRUGGLE

Paul

I have never been homeless in my life
And I am really struggling...
I am really struggling...

If people look at me
I want them to see I'm not happy;
I think if I go on the way I am,
I'm going to die;

I won't be able to survive the winter,
I can't survive...

"You go out in these streets,
there are people dying."

- Paul

CARDBOARD CITY

Ann-Marie, age 10 (Mile Oak Primary)

Here I am again living on hard cold stone...
Here I lie unsafe and scared thinking that I could be
Kicked out by another.

Here I stay thinking there might be no tomorrow and
I may wake in hospital.
I feel scared, unreal and cold and insecure.
Here I have to be alert and awake 24/7.

I can trust no one at all not even an old friend.
I may be robbed or hurt here. I may not eat here.
I am isolated and distinctly lonely, I need a companion.
I have danger everywhere around me; here is my
Cardboard bed.

This place could be a forever home.
Is this the real me!?

ON THE BENCH, I CRIED

Edette

For the first time it was Christmas,
I sat on a bench
At the Pavilion Gardens;
I sat there crying...

8.30am. Saturday morning. David Bolton with Paul by Crossover Brighton's street kitchen, Kitty.

MY EYES... REFLECTION WITH LINDA

Jay, Karl and Angela

In my eyes, you will see colour,
Darkness; you will see a mask,
In my eyes, see the one looking into them,
A story not ended; in my eyes you will see
My story just beginning...

MONOLOGUE (extract)

Freya, age 11 (Mile Oak Primary)

I left not knowing I'd be living on the streets
The next day. I was only nine.
I tied my hair up with ribbon,
Memories came flooding back:

I was gazing into my parents' eyes
After opening my most favourite present – a diary!
That night my mum and dad were arguing,
Yelling at each other. I couldn't bear it!
The next day, after school, no one was at home...

MONOLOGUE IN ZOE'S VOICE (extract)

Chloe, age 11 (Mile Oak Primary)

36 years I've been on the street.
My most prized possession would be myself
For that's all that's left in my life,
And when spoilt children come by saying
What a filthy woman,
I think in my mind what a snobsie.
I felt lucky to find a mirror just chucked away
And I looked at my handsome self.
Also the most proudest thing I thought to do
Is drive people insane. One day,
These teenagers came and saw me
And threw loads of rubbish bags on my head.
My hair was ruined.

"I was told there was no such thing
as homelessness."

– Tat

Peter draws his self-portrait to reflect the man he sees in the mirror of himself.

20

THE TRAVELLER

Jayson

I've been brought up as a traveller.
If I'm indoors,

It feels like the walls are closing in,
And I need to be outside.

Sometimes I sleep outside
Even though I have a place now.

What I need is a trailer,
A caravan.

ATMOSPHERE HERE (extract)

Amelia, age 10 (Mile Oak Primary)

The stones are crunching against my ear...
The atmosphere is rocky,
The ground feels and looks like ashes...maybe it is?
Of all the careers I could be doing,
And I'm here lying on a piece of cardboard.
Still and motionless...

"Out here in the perimeter, there are no stars."

- Ray

A REALITY

Indrek

If I had a job,
I would have a home to live in,
The money coming in there.

"I need an address. But I don't have an address."

- Indrek

A doorway. Cheryl newly awakens — she has the one yellow blanket, she has no coat.

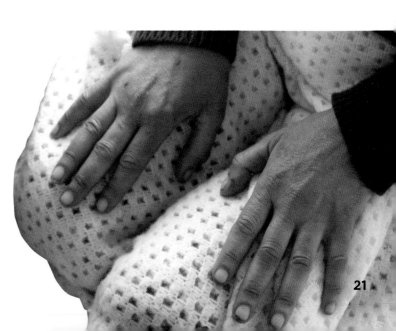

21

STRUGGLES

LIFE JOURNEY

Edette

My experience growing up –
In a family as a Military kid;

But due to a short period
Of circumstances,

I then experienced
What it was like

To have nothing,
And ended up

Sleeping in a tent
For a short period of time;

Everything is
Overseas.

Street people don't get enough money,
And I realise why they steal.

THIS VULNERABLE ME

Hannah V N, age 10 (Mile Oak Primary)
(Front cover poem on cardboard)

I shiver, not because I'm cold,
I shiver with fear.
I'm restless and scared.

Here I have no pillow so I have no sleep.
I use a piece of rubbish for a pillow,
Is this hope?

I have nothing to do but watch.
Watch cars, watch pedestrians.

I feel vulnerable and lonely,
I need a friend.

Here is a home not a house.
I would rob a house nearby.

What do I do now? Talk to myself?
Let's stuff a bag with soft stuff –
At least it's a pillow.

Will the wind blow me away?

The wind keeps blowing
My cardboard away.

I can't remember the day any more.

"If you fall asleep on the streets,
your pockets are emptied..."

– John

Paul receives a pair of socks
from a charity.

CARDBOARD CITY

Luca, age 9 (Mile Oak Primary)

Here I feel comfortable, with lots of other people, but stones dig in to my knees.
In this box of myself, I lie with excruciating pain, day and night.
I can't get to sleep tonight, worry climbs all over me like a curious bug.
As I sit here, a wave of sadness and vulnerability sweeps over my head.
People walk past, drunk and uncaring, without a worry in the world.
When will I finally obtain a proper home?

HELP
ME!

THE WISH

Ray

Night erupts and fills the sky.
I close my eyes and make a wish...

Oh, how I wish...

Catching a lift on the incessant wind,
Riding a tidal wave of darkness,
Letting it carry me on raven's wings
O'er desert and into the void.

I soar o'er barren buttes,
Maroon tablelands
And the buckled and torn mantle
Of Mother Earth...

An earth devoid of city lights.

The land performs a magically spectral transformation
As I repeal the sunset and catch the day once again.

"I am in two worlds at the moment." – Sid

"This bears some thinking about." – Ray

Linda Bolton rummages through a bin at the Old Steine for crushed cans that will transform into a Cross.

23

TO THIS WORLD (extract)

Chloe, age 11 (Mile Oak Primary)

Here I lay sorrowful
Wrapped up with my only piece of cardboard.
Also connected with a pile of stones for my pillow...
My life is worth nothing to this world
For it has given me great misery.

"I've got a lot going on and I don't want
to get emotional."

- Anonymous

A homeless man takes a
moment for a cup of tea.

Gold

Wet

SOULS LOST IN THE VOID

Danny Boy, The Prodigal

Love is not just a feeling
It's an act of your will
Go out and show the world
And give a helping hand
A little hug, and listen
And try to understand
Street children, street children
Everywhere the common
The bullring, the embankment, the square
Poor lost souls
Who don't have a home?
Rejected, unloved
And oh so alone
Do you have a heart?
Do you really care?
Do you have a soul?
Will you be there?

"Asking questions is a challenge for us all. Ask
questions; we are all implied in the struggle."

- Linda Bolton

GRACE

Philippe wears grace on his wrist

"It's not money we want, but just for acceptance, just for acknowledgement."

- Stephen

GRACE

RECOLLECTION OF MY FATHER

Edette

All my Father's money I wasted;
I realise for the first time in my life

How much money I wasted;
As soon as my money was cut

I sold my jewellery.
I wasted so much money;

It was not my money,
It was my Father's...

I had no value...

I just wish in this case my Father was alive,
I'd say, 'Sorry Father, I have wasted all your money.'

I had everything; with his money,
I had diamonds;

I went climbing.
I had no value...

If he was alive,
I would say,

'I am really sorry,
Father.'

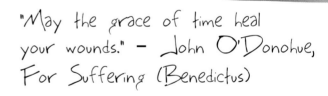

"May the grace of time heal your wounds." – John O'Donohue, For Suffering (Benedictus)

BIBLE QUOTE:

"By this we shall know that we are of the truth and reassure our heart before him..."
– *Bible (English Standard Version), 1 John 3:19*

26

SEEING

Ray

Can you see me?
Can you?

Can you?

Can you hear me, God?
Can you?

Can you?

Do you have big ears, God?
Do you?

Do you?

I don't think they make you look odd.
The walls are only thin

So please, God, let me in.
And safely in your arms keep.

But if you're not here by 9 o'clock
I'm going to sleep.

"I remember a poem I wrote, it was
called *Endurance, journey's end...*"

- Peter

7.30am. Brighton Station.
Alistair kneels on the ground
beside the Crushed Can Cross
made out of tins from the bins.

REMEMBRANCE

Bianka, age 8 (Mile Oak Primary)

I woke up this morning, remembering
The past of a person. He was homeless.

Why was he homeless?
What happened to him?

Is he okay?
How did he get homeless?

I had all those sad thoughts in my head.
I thought I'd find out in the past
But I didn't. Past is past,
And NOTHING can change that!

Is he still homeless?
Is he ok?
Is he alive?

I guess I'll never know...
Is he not homeless?
Is he OK?

What's he doing?
Will I ever find out?
Probably not...

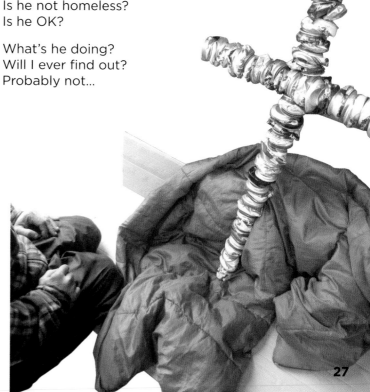

GRACE

MONOLOGUE: FINDING A PLACE

William, age 10 (Mile Oak Primary)

I remember...in the orphanage...
Sharing a room with my best friend, Will,
And the day he got adopted,
And I was on my own.

I remember finding Ben in the pound,
Locked up,
I remember stealing the keys,
And setting him free.

I remember when I found my spot
Under a bridge
Encased by bushes,

And the joy of being able
To call a place my own...

A message from a homeless man written on the cardboard as the Crushed Can Cross takes shape.

QUATRAIN: ON THE WAY

Dermot

No money.
Trust few.
Always paddle
Your own canoe.

COUPLET: VIEW FROM ABOVE

Steven

People can't see us
Because we're above them...

LIFE AND SOUL

Philippe

Words in the Bible
Are pure gold.

I care about
My soul.

This Bible will be
With me

To the end
Of my life.

"I am an ordinary citizen."

- Edette

THE GIFT OF INSIGHT

Edette

Moses was brought up
In a government empire;
Suddenly he was flung out,
In to the desert;

God has given me the same thing –
Thrown me in the gutter,
The pavement –
To give me insight.

PAIN

A touch of gold on the cover
of Philippe's Bible that is so
precious to him.

29

Mile Oak Primary School. The young writer concentrates to reflect on the life of a homeless person and write about his truth.

HERE I LIE

Ellis, age 9 (Mile Oak Primary)

Winter

Here I lie, in the cold,
Here I lie, stones in my back,
Here I lie with all our friends,
Here I lie waiting for a companion,
Here I lie in the damp sleeping bag,
My dreams were crashed!
CRASH.

Spring

Flowers grow, I feel jolly,
I move with my friends,
To a comfy field perhaps,
The grass, comfy.
I walk around feeling dead,
I see corrupt metal
That's my life.

Summer

No need for a bag,
It's so warm,
Waiting around with nothing but trousers.
HELP ME!

Autumn

My hat in tatters.
Nothing left but a soul.
It has gone for ever!

"On the streets, time drags – in a good way."

– John

Love
is
Blind

GRACE

MESSAGE FROM A FATHER

Alistair

My two daughters are precious to me.
I hope they are both doing well,
And the Big Man upstairs
Is watching over them.

I last saw them 26 months ago –
Two years...
February.

What I want to say to them –
Don't listen to others,
Just say, 'No.'

I know how easily led I am,
And if they are 'owt like me,
They would be...

What I want to say –
My daughters are precious,
I would like them to be well educated
And follow their dreams.

BIBLE QUOTE:

"The Lord is close to the broken hearted and saves those who are crushed in spirit." – *Bible (New International Version), Psalm 34:18*

5.30am. Brighton Station. Alistair plays his flute for passers-by.

FAITH

Danny Boy, The Prodigal

I can't remember
How it came
This deep untroubled peace
I only know
One beautiful night
My heart found its release
From all the bondage
Of the past
Its anguish and its fears
And all the hurts
Of yesterday
And all its bitter tears
I only know that fear
Has gone
And every doubt has fled
And faith goes with me
Day by day
Each step I tread

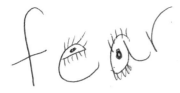

Out of the tins on the streets, Daniel Laurence and Frank DaCosta sculpt the Crushed Can Cross arrayed on Brighton beach where men and women sleep rough.